LA VIDA APASIONADA

Suite for Violin and Piano

Exclusive Distributors for Australia and New Zealand
Encore Music Distributors
6 Abbott St, Alphington. 3078 Victoria Australia
Ph +61 3 9415 6677 Facsimile +61 3 9415 6655
Email sales@encoremusic.com.au

This book © Copyright 2024 by Margaret Brandman trading as Jazzem Music
46 Gerrale St, Cronulla NSW 2230 Australia
ISBN 978-0-949683-05-2

ORDER NUMBER MMP 8149

International Copyright Secured (APRA/AMCOS) All Rights Reserved
Unauthorised reproduction of any part of this publication by any means
including photocopying, is an infringement of copyright.

LA VIDA APASIONADA

Introduction

The duet arrangements in this suite of Latin-American dance style works for violin with piano, are reductions of the ensemble compositions commissioned by Vov Dylan and the Palace Orchestra as chamber works.

The works explore various Latin-American styles including:
Tango, Bossa Nova, Samba, Cha Cha Cha, Argentinian Waltz, Beguine, Bachata, & Rhumba

The violin and piano settings of the suite, have been recorded by Vov Dylan and Margaret Brandman
See pages 87-92 of this book for detailed performance notes and gradings provided by Vov Dylan.

Apart from the violin and piano suite, these works have also been arranged for solo piano and other instruments including 'cello.

Piano backing tracks are available for each of the pieces.
Follow the QR Code below to purchase.

Margaret Brandman
Ph.D Mus/Arts. Hon D.L (IBC)
B.Mus., A.Mus.A., T.Mus.A., Dip E. (WPTA)
'Best Foreign Composer'
Artemis Film Festival Los Angeles
2019 and 2021
Australian Classical and Classical Crossover
Aria charts No1 2023

Follow the QR Code to view the La Vida Apasionada Overture video for free and/or purchase:
1) the complete tracks on the Duo album in either hard copy or digital form
2) the backing tracks in digital form
3) the MP4 Video of the TRIO performance of the suite

Vov Dylan commissioner of the
La Vida Apasionada suite.

https://gig-alliance.com/artist/margaret-brandman/

Contents

1	Tango Apasionada	6
2	Bossa Sonora	13
3	Summer Samba	22
4	Tristeza del Corazón Roto	28
5	Morning Star Cha Cha Cha	38
6	Danza de la Alegría	43
7	Primavera Waltz	49
8	Jucaro Rhumba d'Amor	58
	Violin parts contents page	66
	VIOLIN Parts See p66 for individual page numbers	67-86
	Performance notes by Vov Dylan	87-92

INFORMATION on DANCE STYLES, GRADING and APPROXIMATE DURATION

Australian Music Examinations Board (AMEB) Grades 6-7-8 are advanced grades

	Title	Dance Style	AMEB Grading	Duration
1	**Tango Apasionada**	Tango	6+	3.48
2	**Bossa Sonora**	Bossa Nova	6+	3.38
3	**Summer Samba**	Samba	8+	2:27
4	**Tristeza del Corazón Roto**	Spanish love song	Associate Diploma or above	4:56
5	**Morning Star Cha Cha Cha**	Cha Cha Cha	7+	2:08
6	**Danza de la Alegría**	Beguine, Bachata Boogaloo	7+	3:04
7	**Primavera Waltz**	Argentinian Waltz	7+	2:25
8	**Jucaro Rhumba d'Amor**	Cuban Rhumba	7+	3:31

Refer to the performance notes by Vov Dylan in the last section of this book, for:
1) Technique tips and stylistic insights for each piece
2) Modification suggestions to simplify the pieces and allow the pieces to be performed at a lower grade level. See pages 87-92

INFORMATION on MOOD, TEMPO and KEYS

Title	Mood/Style	Tempo	Key
Tango Apasionada	Dramatic and captivating	Dramatic Rubato introduction Moderato	D minor
Bossa Sonora	Suave and sensuous	Allegretto	C minor with a modulation to D Major
Summer Samba	Bright and breezy in Alla Breve/Cut Common time	Allegretto	E Major
Tristeza del Corazón Roto	Sorrowful, Tender and contemplative	Andante	Descending key structure. Opening in the key of A minor each section modulates to a lower key, first G minor and finally F#minor creating the feeling of sadness of the broken heart
Morning Star Cha Cha Cha	Light-hearted and joyful	Moderato	Ascending key structure. Beginning in D major and rising to E Major
Danza de la Alegría	Bright Beguine, and Bachata rhythms	Moderato	D minor throughout finishing on a joyous Tierce de Picardie (D major chord)
Primavera Waltz	Lively Argentinian Waltz	Allegretto	G minor modulating up a fifth to D minor for the final 20 Bars
Jucaro Rhumba d'Amor	Celebratory Party movement	Moderato	In D minor with contrasting sections in the relative major (F Major)

Tango Apasionada

Margaret Brandman

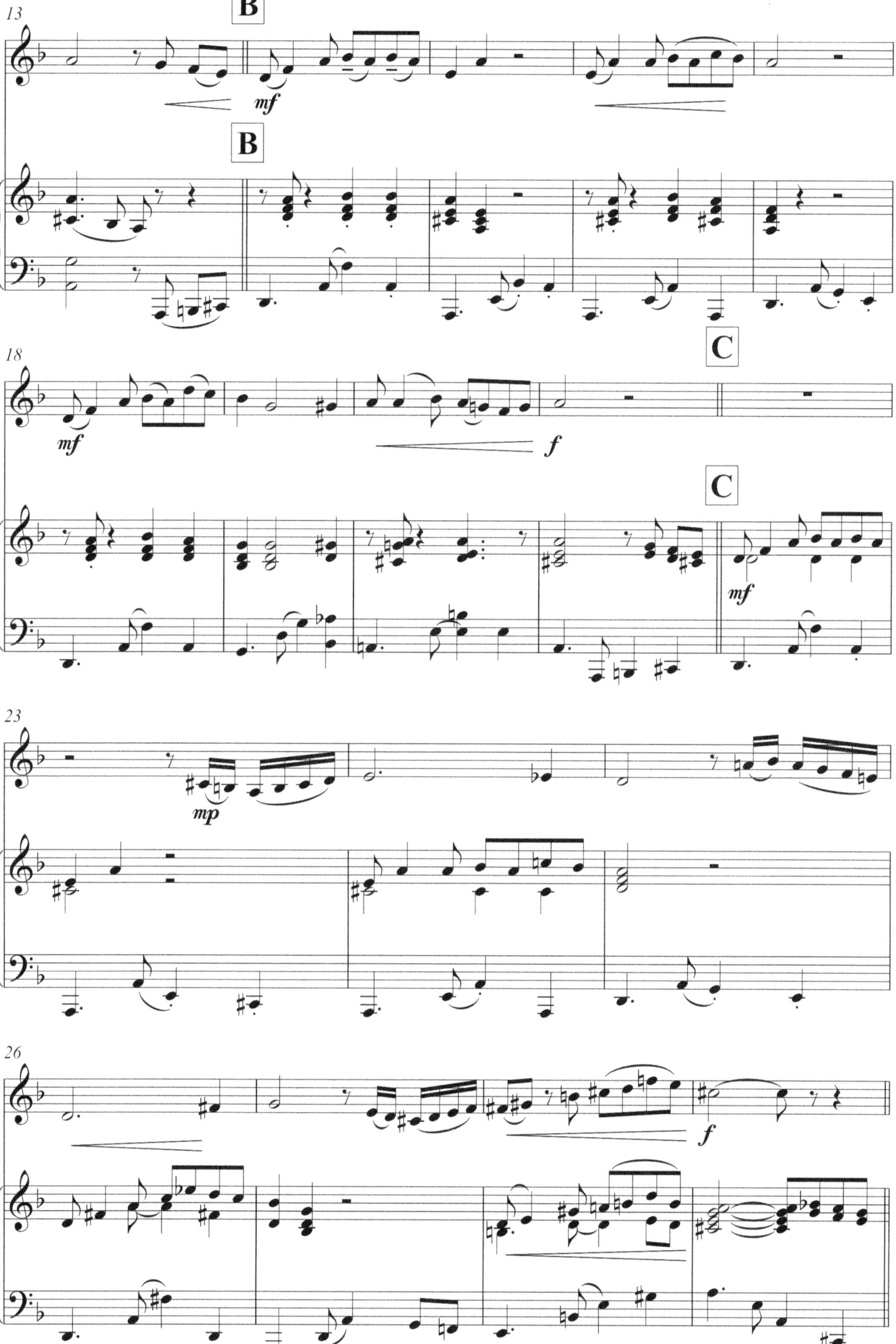
13
B
mf
B
18
C
mf
f
C
mf
23
mp
26
f
-2

8.

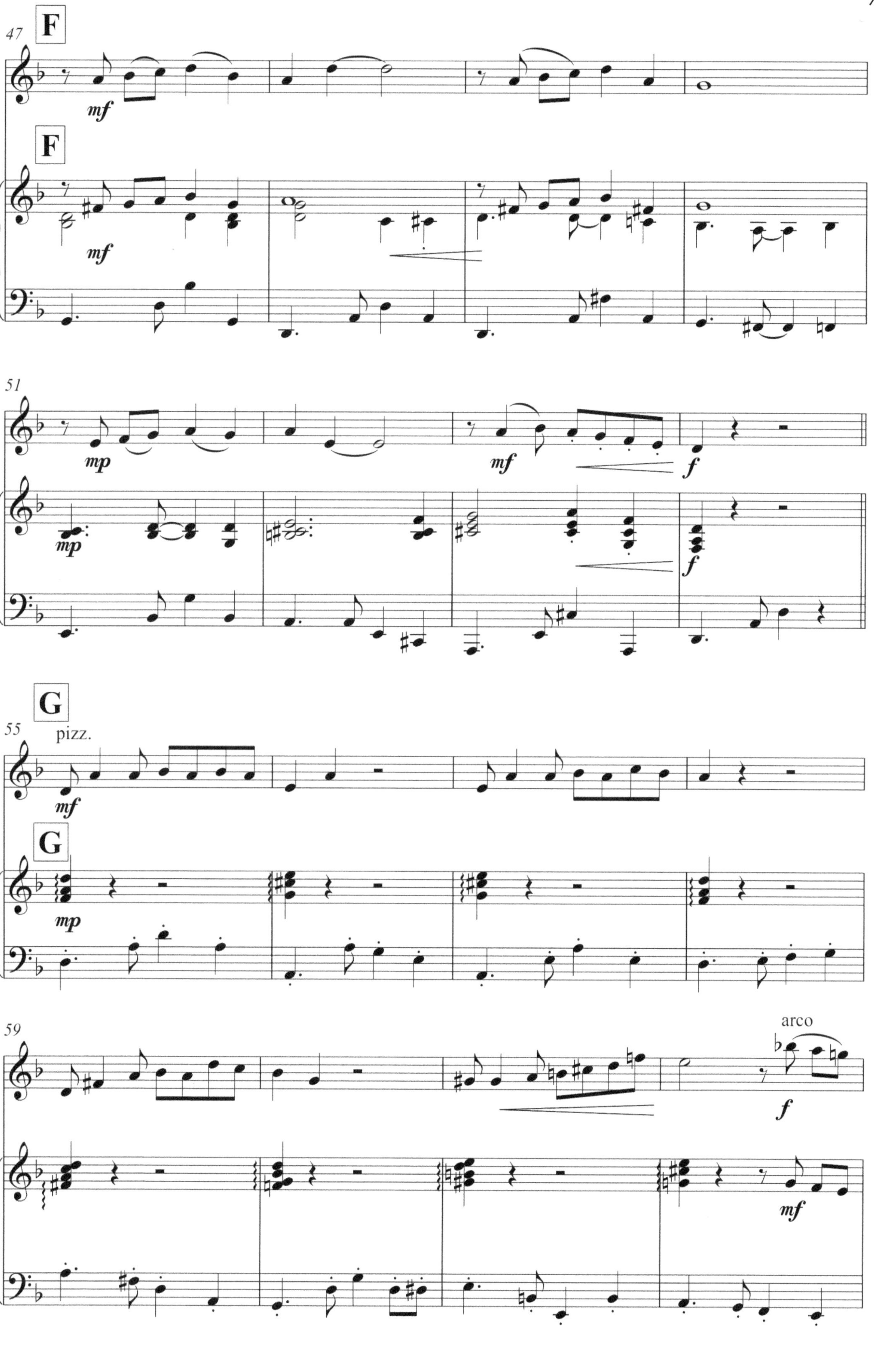
F
47
mf
F
mf
51
mp
mp
mf
f
f
G
55
pizz.
mf
G
mp
59
arco
f
mf

12.

Bossa Sonora

Margaret Brandman

This version © Copyright 2024 Margaret Brandman APRA/AMCOS All Rights Reserved.

14.

16.

18.

20.

Summer Samba

Margaret Brandman

24.

26.

Tristeza del Corazón Roto

Margaret Brandman

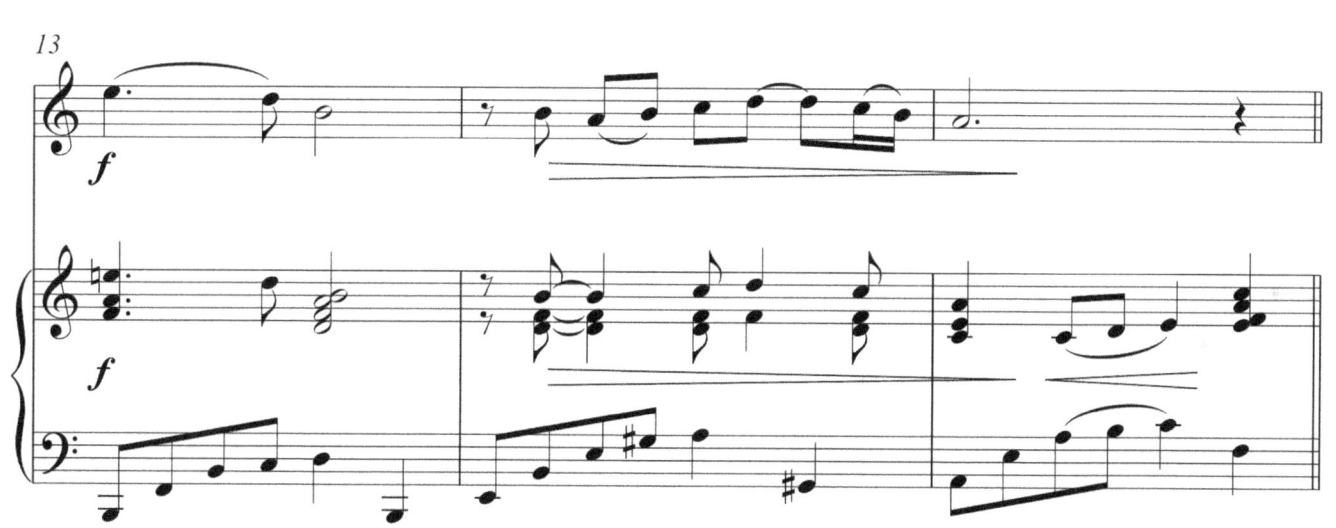

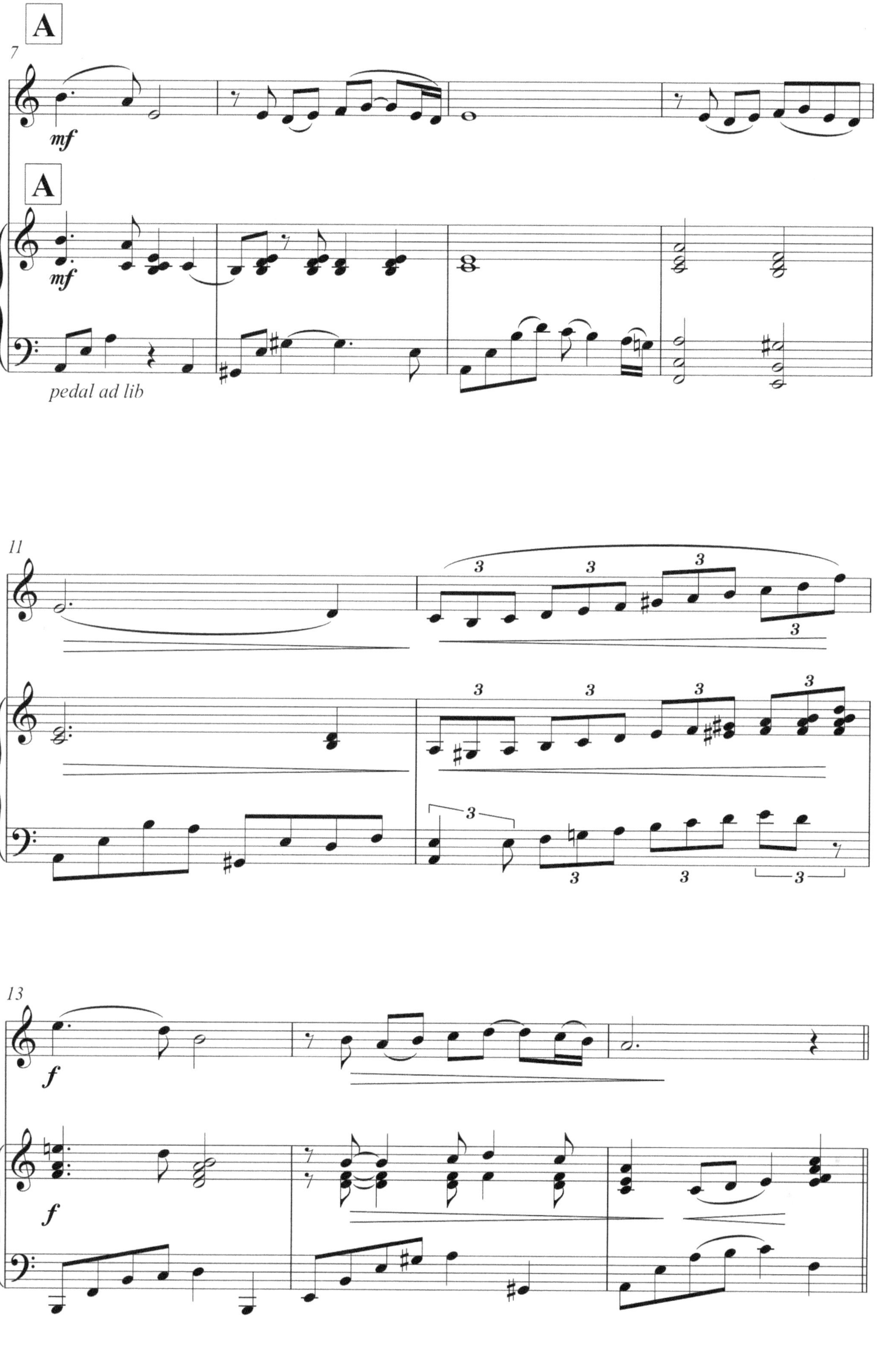
A
7
mf
A
mf
pedal ad lib
11
13
f
f

30.

34.

36.

Morning Star Cha Cha Cha

Margaret Brandman

39.

40.

42.

Danza de la Alegría

Margaret Brandman

44.

48.

Primavera Waltz

Allegretto ♩= 120

Margaret Brandman

This version © Copyright 2024 Margaret Brandman APRA/AMCOS All Rights Reserved.

50.

54.

56.

Jucaro Rhumba d'Amor

Margaret Brandman

64.

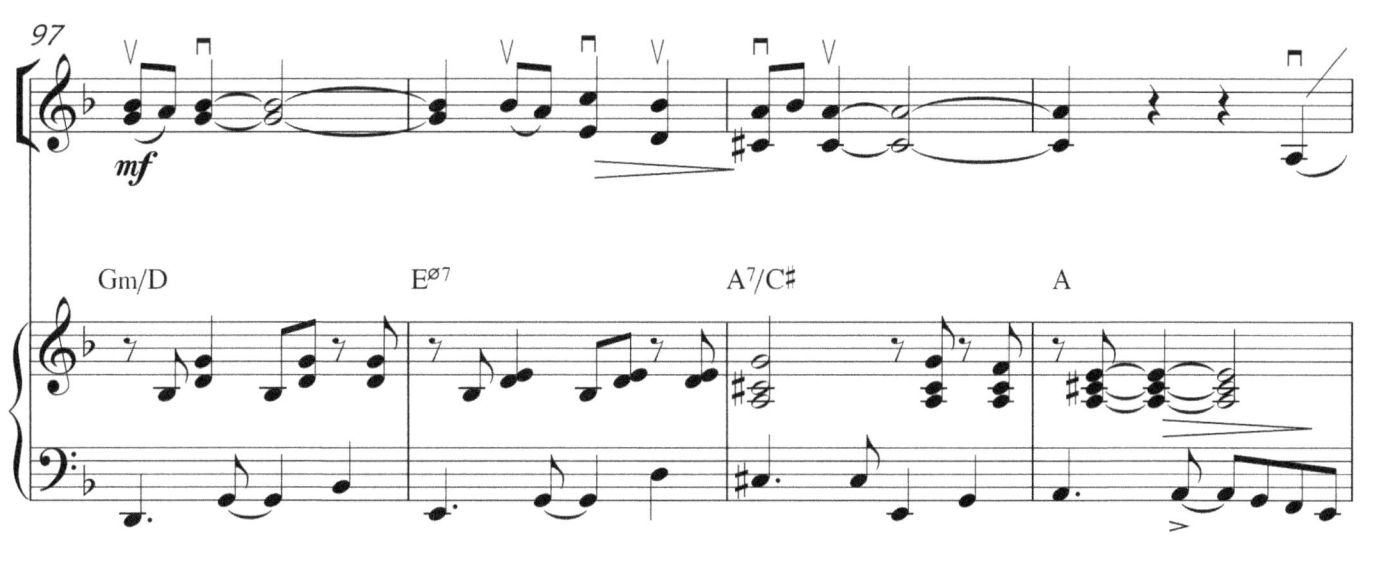

VIOLIN PARTS

1	Tango Apasionada	67
2	Bossa Sonora	70
3	Summer Samba	72
4	Tristeza del Corazón Roto	74
5	Morning Star Cha Cha Cha	78
6	Danza de la Alegría	80
7	Primavera Waltz	82
8	Jucaro Rhumba d'Amor	84

Purchasers of this book are permitted to make a single copy of each violin part for performance purposes.

Alternatively, email the publisher at info@margaretbrandman.com with proof of purchase, to receive a digital copy of the parts.

Violin

Tango Apasionada

Margaret Brandman

Summer Samba

Violin

Margaret Brandman

74.

Violin

Tristeza del Corazón Roto

Margaret Brandman

76.

This page is left blank intentionally

Morning Star Cha Cha Cha

Violin

Margaret Brandman

Violin

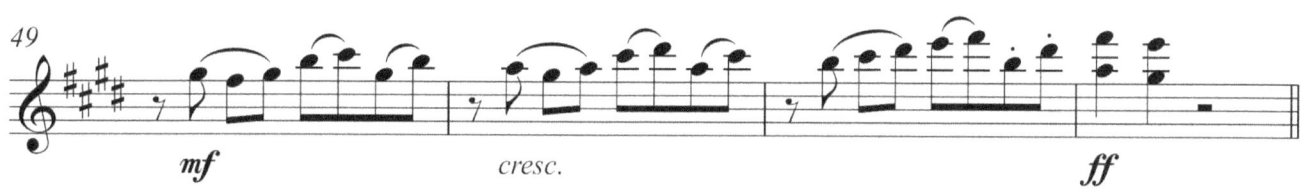

Danza de la Alegría

Violin

Margaret Brandman

PERFORMANCE NOTES
by Vov Dylan

Preface

It is with great honour that I have collaborated with composer Margaret Brandman in the creation of this suite, a journey that commenced with a recording of *Jucaro Rhumba d'Amor* alongside John Martin, leading to the evolution of a friendship and working partnership.

As a performer, my appreciation for *Jucaro Rhumba d'Amor* stemmed from its melodically engaging nature and rhythm that instantaneously prompts movement. The genesis of this suite emerged as an extension of that concept. Fuelled by my request Margaret Brandman composed a suite encompassing diverse Latin rhythms, which, through the sequencing of musical movements, weaves a narrative of love.

Pragmatic considerations played a pivotal role in shaping the musical composition.

These practical elements encompassed:

1. Ensuring the work's duration is conducive to student performances for core Higher School Certificate (HSC) presentations.

2. Crafting individual movements that, while part of a suite, function as standalone compositions.

3. Adaptability of the music for diverse instruments through transposition.

The suite has undergone various adaptations, ranging from small string ensembles to piano trios, culminating in the present Violin and Piano arrangements published in this volume.

Collaborating closely with Margaret Brandman throughout each performance and recording session, has been a source of joy. Notably, the Violin and Piano works within this collection represent the pinnacle of technical complexity among all iterations. She has imbued the violin parts with intricate harmony lines, incorporating multiple double-stop passages and counter melodies, elements that, in larger ensemble versions, are distributed among various instruments.

In an effort to guide performers in interpreting these compositions, I have provided notes that consider both the composer's intent and the performer's individuality, drawing from my collaboration with Margaret Brandman.

Additionally, I have included insights into the musical traditions and styles that have influenced the composition and performance of these pieces. I highly suggest exploring these works in additionto listening to other works by the composer, to help with your own interpretation of these compositions.

Key: AMEB refers to the Australian Music Examinations Board

TANGO APASIONADA

TECHNICAL LEVEL: AMEB Advanced, Grade 6+

This composition is crafted at an advanced technical level, aligning with the proficiency expected at AMEB Grade 6 or above.

Performers wishing to approach this piece at an intermediate level are encouraged to consider the following modifications:

- a) Bars 96: Remove all double stops and mordents.
- b) Bar 102: Play as written instead of using 8va.
- c) Bar 108: Contemplate playing down the octave.

Rooted in the traditional Ballroom Tango tradition, pre-dating the influence of Astor Piazzolla, this work opens with an introduction reminiscent of a Violin Cadenza, akin to those found in compositions like Gade's "Jealousy."

The introduction provides a canvas for the performer to exhibit flamboyance. Feel at liberty to incorporate subtle embellishments and manipulate the timing, seizing the opportunity to establish the ambiance.

Characterised by a pronounced rhythmic quality, it is recommended to place significant emphasis on articulations as indicated in the Violin score. This meticulous attention to articulation will enhance the overall performance, especially in collaboration with the piano.

BOSSA SONORA

TECHNICAL LEVEL: AMEB Advanced, Grade 6+

This composition is meticulously crafted to demand advanced technical proficiency, consistent with the standards expected at an Advanced Grade 6 level and beyond, surpassing the requirements set by the AMEB for Grade 6.

Performers wishing to approach this piece at an intermediate level are advised to consider the following modifications:

- a) Sul Tasto Melody at Letter F: Play the melody down an octave.
- b) Letter G Double Stops: Omit the lower note in the double stops.
- c) Last 3 Bars Harmony: Omit the lower harmonies in the final three bars.

This Bossa Nova draws deeply from the harmonies and rhythms of Brazil, exemplified by the compositions of Antonio Carlos Jobim.

The essence of the piece lies in the chordal progressions within the piano accompaniment.

To navigate the Violin part effectively, performers should adopt a laid-back approach to the beat, resisting the urge to anticipate, especially at Letter C.

For effective practice, it is highly recommended to incorporate a Bossa Nova percussion loop instead of a metronome. This approach, as described by Alexsy Igudesman, facilitates what is termed "Groove Practice," enhancing the rhythmic and stylistic elements of the performance.

SUMMER SAMBA

TECHNICAL LEVEL: AMEB Advanced, Grade 8+

This composition is crafted at an advanced technical level, aligning with the proficiency expected at an AMEB Certificate of Performance level or above, with technical demands from double stop work and off-beat Latin dance rhythms.

Performers wishing to approach this piece at Grade 7 level are advised to consider the following modifications:

    a) Removal of all lower notes in harmonies
    b) Taking the melody line throughout letter H down the octave
    c) Taking the melody from mid bar 85 - mid bar 93 down the octave

This Samba is filled with complex Latin dance rhythms as can be found in many of the pieces made popular by performers such as Xavier Cougar, Perez Prado and Tito Puente.

The complexities of successfully performing this work come in the understanding of the placement of the accents and articulations throughout the work.

Following the slurs and accents as put in the score is vital accurate for performance interpretation.

An added suggestion for bringing contrast, is to change the speed and width of vibrato. For example in bar 1, when looking at the first two crotchets, contrast these by using a fast & narrow vibrato on the first, followed by a fast and wide vibrato on the second.

When looking at the double stop passages employ a fingering that keeps on the same two strings as opposed to slurring across; e.g. in bar 24 and 25 stay on G and D string without use of A string.

To prepare for this piece, practice scales in 3rds, 5ths and 6ths on the G and D strings particularly.

I also suggest doing these scales with a metronome, playing each double stop on the off-beat and feeling the missing quaver/eighth note between the crotchet beats.

TRISTEZA DEL CORAZON ROTO

TECHNICAL LEVEL: Professional or AMEB Associate of Music diploma (A.Mus.A) or above

This demanding work requires facility in multiple technical areas. Simplification of this work is not possible without losing musical integrity.

This work is unique in this suite in that it doesn't have a set dance style as its underpinnings. It is instead written as a free-form style of dance to symbolise heartbreak, featuring multiple downward key changes to reflect new depths of emotion with subtle 'waves of upward melody' to signify hints of hope to come.

Due to the nature of the piece it is recommended to employ the use of downward portamento to portray 'sighs'.

Pay close attention to the time-signature changes and the resulting subtleties that these bring to interpretation of rhythm. For example bars 27 - 31 with triplets compared to 49-51 written with semiquavers/16th notes.

An added technical challenge is that while this piece has multiple time-signature and tempo changes, there needs to be a natural flow and transition where the changing beat emphasis can be understood by a dancer.

For musical interpretation and inspiration, I suggest listening to such works as *El Triste en Vivo*, and some of the slower works by Argentinian composer Astor Piazolla.

This work requires the performer to have both a technical grasp of their instrument and facility for emotional interpretation.

MORNING STAR CHA CHA CHA

TECHNICAL LEVEL: AMEB Advanced, Grade 7 +

This composition is crafted at an advanced technical level, aligning with the proficiency expected at a Grade 7 AMEB (Australian Music Examinations Board) or above.

Performers wishing to approach this piece at an intermediate level are encouraged to consider the following modifications:

    a) Take bars 17 - 20 down the octave
    b) Take Bars 41-44 down the octave
    c) Remove the lower notes in bars 46, 48, 52 and 64

Please note: unlike other works in this collection the double stop passages in letters D and F may not be simplified as these are important harmonies to be maintained.

This playful Cha Cha Cha has its origins in Ballroom Dancing Cha Cha Cha (as opposed to street Latin Cha Cha). This means the emphasis is on the quavers/eighth notes during beat four of the bar leading into beat one of the next bar. Often the Violin and Piano lines trade the "Cha Cha Cha" rhythm pattern. The performers have moments of fun interplay with this "Cha Cha Cha" rhythm is it expressed and changed throughout the work. The key to making this piece a playful and joyful dance is to contrast the articulation for these moments throughout the work.

The music at Letter D is highly contrasted to the rest of the work. Try to make this passage as smooth as possible without excessive articulation. In bar 41 treat this melody as an obligato line, as opposed to a soloist's line.

A tip to help understanding the 'feel' of this work, is for the performers to try to learn how to perform a basic cha cha step.

DANZA DE LA ALEGRIA

TECHNICAL LEVEL: AMEB Advanced, Grade 7+

This composition is crafted at an advanced technical level, aligning with the proficiency expected at AMEB Grade 7 or above.

Performers wishing to approach this piece at an intermediate level are encouraged to consider the following modifications:

    a) Removal of all lower harmony notes.
    b) Taking bars 60-63 down the octave.

This short work is a "Dance of Joy" and is to be interpreted with a lightness to it. This lightness is more important than use of the double stops throughout, so I suggest using these double stops only if they don't interfere with interpretation.

Dance inspirations for this work are: a Beguine which is similar to a slow Rumba, with hints of the Bachata rhythm in the opening section, and for a bit of extra fun and contrast at letter C, a rhythm which is a 1970's New York dance beat known as a Boogaloo. When discussing this work with the composer words that are frequently mentioned are 'Floral', 'Vibrant', 'Playful', and 'Flirtatious.'

For interpretation I highly suggest singing the main melody line and experimenting with portamento to discover areas where the music can breathe. The way this work is written gives the performer lots of scope to find their own sense of cheeky playfulness in the interpretation.

Suggested listening: *Begin the Beguine* by Cole Porter. *Amor* by Gabriel Ruiz

PRIMAVERA WALTZ

TECHNICAL LEVEL: AMEB Advanced, Grade 7 +

This composition is crafted at an advanced technical level, aligning with the proficiency expected at a Grade 7 AMEB (Australian Music Examinations Board) or above.

Performers wishing to approach this piece at an intermediate level are encouraged to consider the following modifications:

    a) Simplification of double stop passages
    b) At bar 98 play this alternate figure.

This is an Argentinian style waltz, which is uniquely different to a Viennese or a ballroom style waltz. In approaching this joyful work it is suggested performers listen to some Argentinian waltzes especially those performed on Bandoneon.

To understand this unique style of waltz, note the example below, which shows emphasis on either beat two of the bar, or the 'and' after the two. Observing these accents will make this magical waltz come alive.

1 + **2** + 3 +   or   1 + 2 **+** 3 +

A performative suggestion is to consider articulation and contrasting vibrato for the first notes of the phrase. A way of finding that right phrasing is to sing/say the word 'Love'. Try to capture the sound of the word while playing these first notes (e.g. the first D from bar 5 into 6, and Bar 35).

JUCARO RHUMBA D'AMOR

TECHNICAL LEVEL: AMEB Advanced, Grade 7 +

This composition is crafted at an advanced technical level, aligning with the proficiency expected at a Grade 7 AMEB (Australian Music Examinations Board) or above.

Performers wishing to approach this piece at an intermediate level are encouraged to consider the following considerations when approaching the double stops:

    a) Either simplification as needed
    b) Permission to 'break the chord' e.g. at letter H play the F for an eighth note/quaver then slur the F and A together.

This work is the only work that was published prior to the creation of this suite of music, and has been published for a variety of instrumental combinations. The performer's focus in this work should be to express the joy of the melody.

This Latin dance rhythm of the Rhumba is further characterised by the composer's familiarity with the Piano Accordion repertoire, for example in bar 85 where the semiquavers/16ths go from being slurred to separated, the musical figure is evocative of the Accordion's 'bellow-shake' technique which creates musical excitement.

The bowing and articulations in this work have been carefully considered by the composer, and are therefore crucial for the interpretation. Having said that, there is scope for the performer to add unwritten elements into the performance. For example consider trying a tremolo technique at letter J, or during the rhythm breaks for solo piano add some percussive elements like taps on the instrument. Try to keep any tempo fluctuations to a minimum as this will break the flow of the work.

Conclusion:

The performance notes for these works are the result of extensive discussions with Dr. Brandman during the composition process, alongside multiple collaborative performances and recordings with the composer.

My main advice to performers is to use these program notes as a starting point for interpretation while developing their own unique approach.

I haven't explicitly mentioned in these notes the influences of jazz and cocktail style performance. Margaret in the writing of this collection has allowed performers the scope (akin to that given to jazz musicians), to explore alternative nuances in interpretation, making each performance fresh and distinct.

While presented as a suite, each composition is designed to be a 'stand-alone' work.

Every work is relatable and tuneful. The music tells the stories of life, love, and emotion.

The added joy is that each composition has been crafted to be approachable and enjoyable alike for both audiences and performers, all of whom are with different tastes and musical inclinations.

I personally have performed these works now in a Classical scenario, in an educational format, and then also with Jazz and Cabaret musicians on stages across the globe and within Australia.

The appeal of the music is instant to performers and audiences!

My hope is that this collection becomes part of the 'fabric of life' where all performers and listeners find joy in these works and revisit them time and time again for years to come.

Vov Dylan
www.vovdylan.com

www.ingramcontent.com/pod-product-compliance
Lightning Source LLC
Chambersburg PA
CBHW082005220426
43669CB00016B/2725